dark blue

D0359056

dark blue

Tudor Exploration

Moira Butterfield

FRANKLIN WATTS
LONDON•SYDNEY

Designer Jason Billin
Editor Sarah Ridley
Art Director Jonathan Hair
Editor-in-Chief John C. Miles
Picture research Diana Morris

First published in 2006
by Franklin Watts
338 Euston Road
London NW1 3BH

Franklin Watts Australia
Hachette Children's Books
Level 17/207 Kent Street
Sydney NSW 2000

ISBN-10: 0 7496 6451 7
ISBN-13: 978 0 7496 6451 0

A CIP catalogue record for this book
is available from the British Library.

Printed in China

Dewey classification number: 910.942'09031

Note to parents and teachers:
Every effort has been made by the Publishers to ensure
that the websites in this book are suitable for children, that
they are of the highest educational value, and that they
contain no inappropriate or offensive material. However,
because of the nature of the Internet, it is impossible to
guarantee that the contents of these sites will not be
altered. We strongly advise that Internet access is
supervised by a responsible adult.

Picture credits
AGE/Superstock: 14.
AKG Images: 22.
Ashmolean Museum/University of Oxford/Bridgeman Art
Library: 18.
Nancy Carter/North Wind Pictures: 4b, 26.
Corporation of London/HIP/Topfoto: 23.
Mary Evans Picture Library: 19, 27.
Guildhall Art Library/City of London/Bridgeman Art
Library: 28.
Kunsthistorisches Museum, Vienna/Bridgeman
Art Library: 16.
Metropolitan Museum, New York/Bridgeman Art Library: 15.
Derek Middleton/FLPA Images: 10.
The National Martime Museum, London: 5t, 6, 8, 12, 13.
Louie Psihoyos/Corbis: 21.
Joel W Rogers/Corbis: front cover, 1, 9t, 17, 29.
Service Historique de la Marine, Vincennes/Bridgeman Art
Library: 3t, 25.
Shawn Spencer-Smith/matthew.co.uk: 7
The Tate, London: 24.
Wellcome Library, London: 11t.
Adam Woolfitt/Corbis: 20.

*Every attempt has been made to clear copyright. Should
there be any inadvertent omission please apply to the
publisher for rectification.*

Contents

The world reveals itself

Tudor kings and queens ruled England for nearly 120 years, from 1485 until 1603. In English history this period of time is called the Tudor Age, but it is also sometimes called the Age of Exploration.

At the beginning of this time, Europeans knew about their own countries and those of their neighbours, but knew very little about the rest of the world. This was to change completely when European sailors began to discover new and mysterious lands.

Silks and spices

What little was known about faraway lands came through trade, the buying and selling of goods through merchants who travelled to Europe from places such as China and the Far East. These merchants charged a lot of money for exotic and expensive items, such as silks and spices, and so became extremely wealthy.

Key fact

A Venetian merchant, Marco Polo, journeyed to China in the 13th century and returned with stories of the magnificent court of the emperor Kublai Khan. Travellers' stories such as his encouraged other Europeans to explore.

Spices such as black and white peppercorns (rear), nutmeg (front left) and cardamom (front right) sold for huge prices in London.

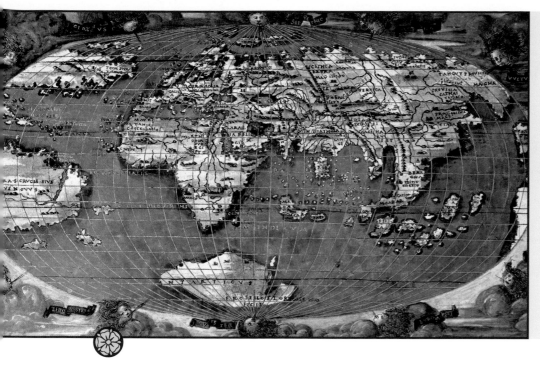

Go and visit

The National Maritime Museum in Greenwich, London is the world's biggest maritime museum. It has lots of seafaring exhibitions and events for children, and a Tudor exploration game on its website www.nmm.ac.uk/.

This map of the world by the map-maker Battista Agnese dates from early Tudor times.

We want that wealth

The important seagoing European nations of the time were Spain, France, Portugal and England. Their monarchs could see how rich the eastern merchants were, and they wanted some of that trading wealth for themselves. They sent sailors to areas where no European seamen had been before, in order to find new goods to sell in Europe.

Indian adventure

The Portuguese were among the first to venture beyond the safety of Europe. Their expeditions sailed down the west coast of Africa and eventually rounded the southernmost tip, the Cape of Good Hope. Vasco da Gama travelled even further to become the first European to sail to India in 1497–98.

Did you know?

Another Portuguese explorer, Ferdinand Magellan, is credited with completing the first voyage around the world between 1519-1522. In fact he was killed part of the way round but one of his ships, the *Vittoria*, did eventually return to Spain with much information about the journey.

Go west!

European sailors and merchants wanted the wealth from the spice trade for themselves so they were keen to find a quick sea route to the Spice Islands of south-east Asia where the spices grew.

For hundreds of years, the spice merchants travelled a slow overland route from south-east Asia, paying customs duty (a tax) on their goods in all the countries they passed through. European sailors knew that it would be much more profitable to sail directly to the Spice Islands (also called the East Indies), to buy the spices themselves and ship them home to sell.

Dangerous sailing
The Portuguese had found a very long route to the Spice Islands around Africa, but it was dangerous. Sailors who tried it endured both terrible storms and pirates, and many never returned home.

A safer short-cut
Sailors in early Tudor times thought that they could find a short cut to the Spice Islands by sailing west across the Atlantic Ocean. They didn't realise that North and South America were in the way, because no complete maps of the world existed.

Did you know?

In 1497 John Cabot was given £10 by Henry VII for discovering the "new-found land". He set off on another expedition in 1498 with five ships and 300 crew, but none of them were ever heard of again.

In Tudor times people believed strange tales about people who lived in faraway lands. They thought, for instance, that there was a tribe of man-eating monsters called *anthropophagi*, who had no heads but had eyes on their shoulders and a mouth on their chest.

We've arrived!

In September 1492, the Italian Christopher Columbus set out on a voyage paid for by King Ferdinand of Spain. Five weeks later he landed safely in the Bahamas, in the Caribbean, which he claimed for Spain. In 1497 John Cabot sailed west from England, backed by the first Tudor king, Henry VII. Seven weeks later, Cabot discovered what he called the "new-found land", part of modern-day Canada. Both thought, mistakenly, that they had discovered islands off the coast of China.

Cabot's original ship, the *Matthew*, was a small light ship known as a caravel.

Go and visit

In 1997 Cabot's ship the *Matthew* was reconstructed to retrace Cabot's voyage. You can visit it sometimes in Bristol harbour, where the original ship began its journey. When the ship is in the port you can go on board and even sail around the harbour on it.

Ships improve

Before the Age of Exploration trading ships had been sailing around the coasts of Europe for many centuries, but without ever going too far out of sight of land.

Sailing the open ocean was more difficult and dangerous, and required a better design of ship. This came from the shipbuilders of Spain and Portugal who developed a large sailing ship with a deeper hold to carry supplies and trading goods. Northern Europeans called this ship a carrack.

Key fact

It took hundreds of oak trees to build a carrack (below). These were transported from forests to the important shipyards where the vessels were constructed.

Go and visit

At the National Maritime Museum in Falmouth, Cornwall, you can find out about sailing boats and their rigging (right), and stand next to some famous ones. You can reach the museum by ferry, and also sail to a nearby Tudor fort built by Henry VIII to guard against foreign invasion.

New-style steering

Originally, medieval ships were pointed at both ends and were steered by a large oar which hung over one side. The carrack carried lots of cargo which made it heavy and difficult to steer, so the steering oar was replaced by a rudder attached to the stern (the back) of the ship. To fit the rudder (a vertical piece of wood), the stern was made flat instead of pointed.

Did you know?

The right hand side of a ship is called the starboard side. This is because the steering oar (also called the steere-board) was always on the right hand side of a ship. When steering oars were replaced by rudders, the name "starboard" still stuck.

Stronger in a storm

A carrack had a wooden framework that was stronger than previous ship designs. It was fixed on to a long timber, the "keel", cut from one tree. The keel ran along the length of the hull like a backbone. The planks of the hull were attached to the frame with long nails. Older ships had planks that overlapped each other but the new-style ships' planks did not overlap and this made them stronger and more rigid.

Clever sails

A carrack normally had three masts to carry its sails. The front and middle mast carried square sails and the mast at the back had a triangular sail. Ropes called "rigging" were fitted to the masts and also to the sails. Older ship designs had fixed sails but carrack sails could be swung around to catch the wind whichever way it blew.

A tough trip

Life on board a Tudor ship was hard at the best of times. When adventurers began to make longer journeys, the conditions got even harsher.

They set sail with no idea how long they would be at sea, or when they would next see land again. There was no escape from storms in the open ocean and no hope of rescue if a ship ran into trouble.

Small for sailors

Although they were sturdy, many Tudor ships were very small. John Cabot's ship, the *Matthew,* was only 20 metres long and six metres wide. Conditions on board were cramped. The *Matthew* had to sail across the stormy Atlantic with a crew of just 18 sailors, all it could fit in. Such a small crew would have had to work very hard to control the ship on the voyage.

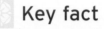 **Key fact**

The *Matthew* was at sea for seven weeks on its voyage across the Atlantic. Luckily, the sailors were able to supplement their diet with fish. They found the sea so rich in cod they could catch them just by putting baskets into the water.

Rats infested 16th-century ships. They ate the sailors' food supplies and gnawed their way through ropes and other equipment.

Go and visit

The *Mary Rose* in Portsmouth, Henry VIII's favourite warship. It sank in 1545 but was rediscovered, raised and partly put back together. You can see the sailors' belongings, found near the wreck, and find out about life on a Tudor ship.

By *his* M A ƒ E S T I E S Licence,

A Book of Directions

And Cures done by that Safe and Succesful Medicine CALLED,

AN

HERCULEON ANTIDOTE,

OR THE

GERMAN GOLDEN ELIXIR

V.Which is defervedly fo called, for its Special Virtues, in Curing that
POPULAR DISEASE, the *SCURVEY.*

THIS HERCULEON ANTIDOTE, Cures by cleanfing of the
Blood, Purging by URINE, and gently by STOOL.

SOme Difeafes are Fami-
liar to fome Nations, which
others are free from ; the *Le-
profie, Itch, Pox,* as in *Italy,*
and fome Parts of the *Indies* ;
fo in the *Eaftern* Parts , our
Popular Difeafe is the *Scurvey,* which this Golden Elixir
hath had fuch admirable Suc-
cefs far beyond any thing Ex-
ftant for the *Scurvey,* and that
it cures moft Diftempers, for
there are few Difeafes , but
has a fpice of the *Scurvey,*
which corrupts the Blood.

The Symptoms and Nature of the Scurvey.

THe Scurvy is the Original of moft violent Diftempers, which this Golden
Elixir preventeth, as Stoppages, Obftructions, raifing Vapours tha-
caufes Swimming and Fumes in the Head, Dimnefs of Sight, Deafnefs, an.
Drowfinefs which makes the Body dull and heavy, and alters the Complexi-
A   on :

Salt and maggots

There was not much space to store food on board and there was no refrigeration or canning of food at the time to help preserve it. The only way to keep food from rotting was to soak it in salt, so sailors survived on a boring diet of salted meat. They also ate ship's biscuit, a type of bread made from flour and water and then baked hard. Often, the salted meat went off and the ship's biscuits became infested with maggots and beetles.

Rats and scurvy

Illness and disease were common on board ship. Most ships had rats living on them, carrying diseases and fouling the food stores. Many sailors died from a terrible illness called scurvy, caused by a lack of Vitamin C, which is found in fresh fruit and vegetables. These foods were not available on a voyage far from land. Scurvy caused sailors' teeth to fall out, long-healed wounds to open and extensive bleeding. At the time, nobody understood the cause of scurvy.

Did you know?

Seafarers struggled with scurvy for hundreds of years and, on long voyages, many captains lost hundreds of men to the disease. "Cures" abounded (above) but the true cure (Vitamin C) was not discovered until the late 1700s.

Finding the way

The sailors of the Tudor Age would have known all the landmarks around their local coast, so it would have been easy for them to know roughly where they were on a local journey.

But on the open ocean there were vast stretches of sea with no landmarks at all, so they had to find new ways to work out where they were.

Minus a map

There were no reliable maps for explorers to use at this time, since many of the lands they came across had never before been visited by Europeans. Map-makers were only able to start drawing accurate charts when the explorers returned from their voyages with information on what they had found.

Instruments such as the astrolabe helped early seafarers to find their way. It helped them to work out the ship's latitude – its position north or south of the equator.

North or south

The magnetic compass (right) was the main navigational instrument on board ship at this time. It contained a magnetised metal needle which always pointed towards the north. Under the needle the compass was marked north, south, east and west, with lots of other direction points marked in between.

By the stars and sun

A ship's captain, or experienced members of his crew, would have done the navigation on a journey. His compass would have told him roughly which way he was travelling, but it couldn't tell him where he was. For this he had to use a measuring instrument such as an astrolabe or a cross-staff to work out the angle between the horizon and either the sun or a particular star that he knew. From there he could work out how far north or south his ship was (its "latitude"). The captain also measured the speed of the ship to estimate how far they had travelled that day.

The Queen's pirates

By the middle of the 1500s Spain had become an enemy of England, because England had turned away from the Catholic religion. Spain was bringing lots of treasures back from its newly discovered lands in Central and South America, and English sailors attacked and stole from the Spanish ships on their way home.

W hilst hunting the ocean for their Spanish enemies, the English got more and more experienced at sailing the open ocean, and even discovered new lands for themselves.

Keep out!

When sailors discovered new land, they claimed it in the name of whichever monarch had helped to pay for their voyage. Although he was Italian himself, Christopher Columbus was backed by the Spanish, so the lands he discovered in the Caribbean and Central America became Spanish. Other Spanish adventurers soon discovered the fabulous treasures of the Aztec and Inca empires, as well as gold and silver mines. Spain was very keen that nobody else should be allowed to benefit from the wealth it found there, so it banned ships from other nations.

A religious object made from South American gold.

Did you know?

Once a year the Spanish sent a fleet of a hundred ships, called galleons, home from the Spanish colonies, carrying treasure from its gold and silver mines.

During his four voyages, Columbus claimed many lands in Central and South America for Spain.

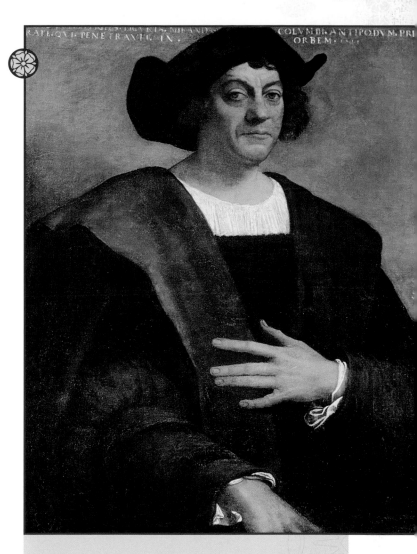

Official pirates

Queen Elizabeth I heard of the new Spanish wealth and wanted some of it for England. So, she granted English sailors an official licence to attack Spanish shipping and settlements abroad, in return for a cut of the stolen treasure. These licensed pirates were called privateers. Whilst on their search for Spanish riches to steal they got used to sailing across the Atlantic and around the coasts of the "'Spanish Main", as the Spanish colonies were called.

Key fact

Sending sailors across the Atlantic as privateers (pirates) was a cheap way for Queen Elizabeth to fight the Spanish, make some profit and possibly discover new lands at the same time.

Did you know?

Seville Cathedral, Spain, houses Christopher Columbus's official tomb, and a huge solid gold altar. If you visit any large church in Spain you are likely to find fabulous treasures made from gold and silver brought home from Central and South America.

Adventurers abroad

The English saw how rich the Spanish were getting, and realised that having foreign colonies abroad could bring enormous wealth back to the country. The privateers were adventurers and experienced seamen, so they were the ideal people to seek out new lands. Elizabeth encouraged them to go exploring.

Drake around the world

Sir Francis Drake is the best-known English sailor and explorer of the Tudor Age. He is famous for his exploits in fighting the Spanish, but he also led the second expedition to sail completely around the world.

I t made him enormously wealthy, and helped to open up world trade for England. On his return Queen Elizabeth I knighted him on board his ship the *Golden Hind* in 1581.

Sailing against the Spanish

Drake was born into an ordinary Devon family. He began his career sailing with his relative, John Hawkins. They sailed to the Caribbean to trade, but then went on privateering raids against the Spanish. Francis Drake's voyage around the globe was planned as another plundering trip. He set off with five ships and 164 men in 1577, but by the time he sailed round the southern tip of South America he only had the *Golden Hind* and 58 men left.

All the way around

On the way, Francis Drake raided Spanish settlements in Peru and Chile and captured Spanish treasure ships. Then, because he thought Spanish ships might be chasing him, he continued to sail west through the Spice Islands, bought spices and sailed on home to Plymouth. His voyage took three years.

Did you know?

Sir Francis Drake was a pirate, an explorer, a slave trader and a national hero, whose clever tactics against the Spanish Armada in 1588 saved England from Spanish invasion.

Voyage of death

During the trip Drake and his crew endured awful conditions. The most difficult time came trying to sail round South America through the Strait of Magellan, when the crew had to survive on penguin and seal meat. Some men died of disease; others from the cold. The other ships in his fleet were lost, beached or were forced to return home.

Key fact

The *Golden Hind* seems very tiny to have made such a long journey. It measured only 37 metres long. Yet when Drake returned, it was loaded with the modern-day equivalent of about £25 million worth of treasure and spices!

Go and see

A full-sized reconstruction of Sir Francis Drake's ship the *Golden Hind*, moored in Brixham, Devon. Climb onboard and find out about the incredible world journey that Drake and his crew experienced.

The route north

By the mid-1500s, European sailors knew that there was a south-eastern route to the Spice Islands (around the tip of southern Africa) and a south-western route (around the tip of South America).

They firmly believed that there must also be north-western and north-eastern routes. Looking for these routes cost many lives.

The north-west passage

Martin Frobisher was a privateer and explorer who sailed towards North America in the hope of finding a way through to the Far East. He was also hoping to find gold. He set out on three voyages between 1576 and 1578, but was forced to return each time as his route was blocked by ice.

A model of an Elizabethan merchantman, a type of ship used by merchants and explorers alike.

Another try

Five years later, another English explorer, Sir Humphrey Gilbert, led an expedition across the North Atlantic. He landed in the area of Newfoundland and established an English colony. Then Gilbert carried on to explore the coastline before returning home. Unfortunately, he died when his ship sank in the Atlantic.

Did you know?

Frobisher brought back large quantities of stone from his trips, believing it to contain gold. But the "gold" turned out to be gold-coloured iron pyrites, a worthless mineral that is nicknamed "fool's gold".

The search north-east

Sebastian Cabot, John's son, raised money for an expedition to search for a north-east route to China. Led by Sir Hugh Willoughby and Richard Chancellor, the ships set off in 1553 to sail around the north of Norway. The expedition landed in Russia and Chancellor travelled overland to Moscow where he established trade links with Russia. Willoughby and his crews froze to death so neither of them ever found the short sea route they were looking for.

Tudor sailors voyaging in the Arctic faced the prospect of a cold death thousands of kilometres from home.

The slave trade

The slave trade grew as a result of the discovery and settlement of new lands. Slave traders found that there was a big demand for slave labour in the new colonies.

At first the Spanish settlers used the native people of the lands that they had taken over to work as labourers, either mining gold and silver or labouring on large sugar cane plantations. They treated them with great cruelty and saw them as little better than animals. Working and living conditions were so bad that many of them died. So new workers were constantly in demand.

A human cargo
To satisfy the demand for labour, traders transported people from the West African coast. Men, women and children were captured by local slaving parties and sold to the traders, who took them to the Caribbean. Here the Africans were sold as slaves in return for goods that could be taken home and sold for a profit.

Manacles like these were used to chain the hands of slaves together, to stop them from escaping.

Did you know?

Sir Francis Drake was one of the first English slave traders. Together with his relative, John Hawkins, he made a number of successful and profitable trips to sell slaves to the Spanish.

Terrible trip

The African slaves were transported across the Atlantic in terrible conditions. They were chained together and packed shoulder-to-shoulder below decks. They had little food and water and many died of starvation and disease before they reached land. Prospects were no better when they got to the Caribbean where their new owners forced them to work until they died. Slaves were not free to leave a cruel owner, were given no pay and only just enough food to survive.

This engraving shows African slaves packed together like items of cargo in a ship's hold.

Key fact

The slave trade has left its mark on the Caribbean right up to the present day. About 80% of the Caribbean community are descended from slaves brought over from Africa.

Go and visit

Bristol Indust   Museum, by the waters of Bristol Harbour. Find out how the slave trad   after it was begun in Tudor times, what conditions were like for the sla   , and how the slave trade was finally stopped in Britain.

Home ports

London and Bristol were the two most important sea ports in England in Tudor times. The increase in overseas exploration and trade made some of the merchants based in these ports very wealthy.

Merchants made big profits from selling the goods their ships brought home from foreign lands.

Ports get bigger

All the goods which came in to England from abroad had to be landed on official quays (areas where ships moored and unloaded). There the government charged the merchants customs duty (a government tax) on the goods. Queen Elizabeth I licensed 20 quays all along the River Thames, between London Bridge and the Tower of London, to carry out this work. These became known as "the legal quays" and ships queued up to land goods there.

Tudor merchants in London plan a voyage. They stood to make a lot of money, but there were also great risks.

Tower Wharfe

S. Olafe

Hustle and bustle

Tudor ports were busy places. The picture above shows the part of the Thames near the legal quays, which was always crammed with shipping. Suppliers of ropes, sails and ships' supplies set up shop along the docksides. Sailors unloaded and loaded cargoes, or spent their wages in dockside inns. Merchants had grand houses built on the profits they made, usually in positions where they could see what was going on in the harbour.

Making money

Overseas voyages could be very profitable, but if a ship sank the people who owned it would lose everything. Groups of merchants and investors began to get together to form companies called joint stock companies, which put up the money for voyages and shared out the profits and the costs of failure. Elizabeth I was an early investor.

Go and visit

Visit your local sailing club to try your hand at river or ocean sailing. If you don't live on the coast or near a river, many clubs are situated on inland reservoirs or lakes and offer lessons in sailing and water safety. Look for information at your local library.

Key fact

The success of the Tudor joint stock companies was the start of London becoming an important world centre of financial deals.

Sir Walter Raleigh

Sir Walter Raleigh (or Ralegh) was a favourite courtier of Queen Elizabeth and one of the most famous celebrities of his day.

Raleigh started an English colony in the country we now call the United States of America and organised the first scientific expedition. He impressed the Queen and won fame for himself, but later on royal displeasure cost him his life.

Raleigh rises

Just like Sir Francis Drake, Raleigh came from Devon, so he was familiar with the sea from childhood. He was a half brother of Gilbert (see page 18) and, like him, decided to organise voyages to North America, thinking he could mine gold there.

This famous Victorian painting - *The Boyhood of Raleigh* - by Millais shows the young Walter listening to tales of the sea, and of new lands.

 Did you know?

Elizabeth I thought that exploring was too risky for one of her most important courtiers, so Raleigh was not allowed to go on many voyages he organised during her reign.

This Elizabethan map shows the doomed colony of "Virginia".

Raleigh is said to have been out walking with the Court when he first impressed the Queen by laying his expensive cloak in a puddle so that she would not have to step in the dirt. Nobody knows if this famous story is true, but he did have a picture of a cloak on his coat-of-arms.

Sending ships to North America
In 1585, Raleigh sent five ships loaded with people to set up a colony on the east coast of America. He called the area "Virginia" after Elizabeth, who was called "the Virgin Queen". At first the new settlers were welcomed by the Native Americans they found, but then the settlers grew short of supplies and stole from the locals. Soon there was fighting and the colony was destroyed. After this initial setback more settlers gradually followed where Raleigh's ships had led.

Go and visit

The Tower of London where Raleigh was imprisoned twice. The second time he had fallen out of favour with James I, who had Raleigh beheaded in the grounds of the Tower.

Key fact

Raleigh's crew brought back the potato to Britain for the first time, along with tobacco. Raleigh then made smoking a pipe fashionable at Court. People thought it was good for the lungs.

25

Bringing home surprises

Tudor explorers brought back not just gold and slaves, but new foods which nobody had seen before.

Today, many of the spices, fruits and other foods we buy in the shops have travelled by air to reach us, the consumers. In Tudor times these products had to come on a long and perilous journey by sea. Sailors also brought back incredible tales of the strange sights they had seen on their travels.

Expensive treats

Spices from the Spice Islands, such as pepper and nutmeg, were highly prized. It was hard to keep food fresh in Tudor times, and the strong taste of the spices helped to hide the taste of stale and rotting food. Some of the spices were also used as medicine. For instance, nutmeg was used to treat stomach problems. Spices were very expensive, so they were mostly used by wealthy people.

A scene in the Banda Islands, where nutmeg grew in Tudor times.

26

This engraving depicts the tale of Sir Walter being "put out" by his servant.

New food

Tobacco, potatoes, maize (corn on the cob), tomatoes and pineapple were introduced into England for the first time by explorers returning from the Americas. Sir Francis Drake brought back a coconut from his trip around the world and presented it to Queen Elizabeth, who had never seen one before.

New sights

Explorers in Tudor times took dangerous journeys into the unknown, and brought back fantastic tales of what they found. For instance, in the Spice Islands they had to dodge fierce head-hunting cannibals and in North America they had to fight man-eating polar bears. Some returning sailors wrote about what they had seen, but sometimes the tales sounded so strange that nobody believed them! Others brought back valuable information about the lands and seas they'd travelled through, which helped map-makers to create much more accurate world maps.

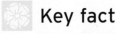

Key fact

Raleigh sent an artist called John White on the voyage of 1585. White painted images of Native Americans and of wildlife never before seen in Europe.

Go and visit

The Pitt Rivers Museum in Oxford, which displays weird and wonderful objects brought back to England from all over the world over centuries of exploration and travel.

Exploration speeds up

By the end of Tudor times, Europeans knew a lot more about the world, thanks to the skill and courage of seamen such as Cabot and Drake, with their sturdy little ships and brave risk-taking crews. But their voyages were only the start.

The pace of exploration began to increase, as European countries searched for more new lands to claim.

British sailing power

The seamanship developed by the Elizabethan explorers enabled Britain to become the top naval power in the world for three centuries. Ship design and naval warfare tactics all improved as a result of the lessons they learned sailing the open ocean looking for new lands, or attacking their enemies to steal their cargoes.

Queen Elizabeth visits the Royal Exchange in London. This was built by the wealthy Sir Thomas Gresham in 1571 as a place for merchants to negotiate deals.

Key fact

The Tudor Age ended with the death of Elizabeth I in 1603. She died childless, so the throne went to her relative James Stuart. The money she had made from exploration and privateering was all spent by the time of her death, and James inherited a government that was virtually penniless.

Merchants get rich

Before the Tudor period, only the nobles and the Church were wealthy in England. Their wealth came from owning farmland. But with the increase in trade overseas, town-dwelling merchants began to get richer, and they eventually began to use their new-found wealth to get more power for themselves.

An empire grows

The quest to discover wealth in new lands laid the foundation for the British Empire, which grew to its largest extent in the reign of Queen Victoria. Soon Britain had many new colonies abroad, and was making lots of money from them. It developed a powerful navy to protect its colonies and its trade routes from enemies.

Did you know?

Elizabeth's successor, James I, sent ships – like the one shown above – to find out what had happened to the settlers Sir Walter Raleigh's expedition had left in Virginia. They found no-one, but later a group of pale-skinned grey-eyed Native Americans was found, possibly the descendants of captured settlers.

Go and visit

Somewhere you have never been before and know nothing about. That way you can imagine what it might have been like to be a Tudor sailor going on a voyage into the unknown!

GLOSSARY

astrolabe
An instrument used on board a ship to work out its latitude, its location north or south of the equator.

carrack
A three-masted cargo ship used in Tudor times, with a rudder for steering and a flat-shaped stern (back).

colony
A settlement set up in a foreign land.

compass
An instrument used to navigate on a journey. It contains a magnetic needle that always points north.

courtier
A noble person who personally served the king or queen of the time.

cross-staff
A navigational instrument used for measuring latitude.

customs duty
A tax paid to a government on goods that are brought into a country.

hull
The framework of a ship.

joint stock company
A group of people who paid for a ship's voyage, and then took a share of the profits or losses made by the venture.

keel
The large timber "backbone" that runs the length of the bottom of a wooden ship's hull.

latitude
The location north or south of the equator.

maritime
To do with the sea.

merchant
Someone who buys and sells goods.

monarch
A king or queen.

navigation
Finding your way on a journey, by working out where you are and which direction you should go.

plantations
Huge crop-growing farms. From the 1600s to the 1860s plantations in America and the Caribbean were worked by slaves.

port
A town or city with a harbour by the sea or by a deep river, where ships dock to load and unload.

privateer
A sea captain licensed by Elizabeth I to attack the ships and colonies of England's enemies.

rigging
The ropes used to control the sails on a sailing ship.

scurvy
A fatal disease which sailors suffered, caused by lack of Vitamin C.

ship's biscuit
A type of bread eaten onboard ships. It was made from flour and water, baked hard.

slave trade
The kidnapping of Africans who were sold to traders and transported to the Caribbean to be sold on as slaves.

spices
Aromatic plants and seeds used in cooking and medicine.

Spice Islands
The islands of south-east Asia, also called the East Indies, where spices grow.

trade
The buying and selling of goods, such as spices and silk.

Tudor
The period between 1485 until 1603, when kings and queens of the Tudor family ruled England.

TIMELINE

1485 Henry Tudor becomes King Henry VII and the Tudor period begins.

1492 Christopher Columbus sets sail to find a route west to the Spice Islands.

1497 John Cabot sets sail to find a route west to the Spice Islands.

1497-8 Portuguese Vasco da Gama and his crew become the first Europeans to sail to India.

1509 Henry VII dies. His son, Prince Henry, is crowned King Henry VIII.

1519 Ferdinand Magellan of Portugal and his crew set sail to become the first crew to sail around the world (Magellan dies on the way home).

1533-34 The English Church breaks away from the Roman Catholic Church; Roman Catholic Spain and France become England's enemies.

1545 The *Mary Rose* sinks.

1547 Death of Henry VIII. He is succeeded by his son Edward VI.

1553 Edward VI dies and is succeeded by Mary I, his sister.

1558 Mary dies and is succeeded by Elizabeth I, her sister.

1576 Martin Frobisher sets sail to find a north-west passage to the Spice Islands.

1577 Francis Drake sets sail from England on a voyage that will end in him going all the way around the world.

1581 Francis Drake is knighted by Elizabeth I onboard the *Golden Hind*.

1583 Sir Humphrey Gilbert founds a settlement in Newfoundland (off the north-east coast of North America).

1585 Sir Walter Raleigh's settlers claim "Virginia" in North America for Elizabeth I.

1588 The Armada, a failed naval invasion of England by Spain.

1603 Elizabeth I dies. She is succeeded by her closest relative James Stuart.

1618 Sir Walter Raleigh is executed.

WEBSITES

www.nmm.ac.uk
The website of the National Maritime Museum in Greenwich, London. Go to "kid's stuff" to find out all about being a Tudor explorer.

www.nmmc.co.uk
The website of the National Maritime Museum in Falmouth, Cornwall. Build a boat in an interactive game.

www.goldenhind.co.uk
See photographs of the reconstruction of Sir Francis Drake's ship the *Golden Hind*, and find out about life onboard.

www.maryrose.org
Find out about the *Mary Rose* exhibition. Take a virtual tour of the ship and meet the crew.

www.matthew.co.uk
See photographs of the reconstruction of John Cabot's ship the *Matthew*, and find out about its history.

www.museumoflondon.org.uk
Go to the learning section and then to the Tudor section for some fun activities and facts on Tudor life in London.

www.portcities.org.uk
Go to the Bristol section of the site to find out more about the slave trade.

INDEX